FORBIDDEN FRUIT

FORBIDDEN FRUIT

MEDITATIONS ON SCIENCE, TECHNOLOGY, AND NATURAL HISTORY

HEATHCOTE WILLIAMS

HUXLEY SCIENTIFIC PRESS
OXFORD

Published by Huxley Scientific Press
35 Marston Street, Oxford OX4 1JU, UK
www.huxleyscientific.com

First published 2011

ISBN 978-0-9522671-5-7

Typeset in Monotype Plantin by the Geometric Press, Oxford
Cover design by Pete Rozycki: www.peterozycki.com
Printed in the UK by Information Press, Eynsham, Oxford

CONTENTS

Biographical history, as taught in our public schools, is still largely a history of boneheads: ridiculous kings and queens, paranoid political leaders, compulsive voyagers, ignorant generals—the flotsam and jetsam of historical currents. The men who radically altered history, the great scientists and mathematicians, are seldom mentioned, if at all.

—Martin Gardner, Book review, *New York Times*, 9 May 1976

The benefits of medical research are real, but so are the potential horrors of genetic engineering and embryo manipulation. We devise heart transplants, but do little for the 15 million who die annually of malnutrition and related diseases. Our cleverness has grown prodigiously—but not our wisdom.

—Sir Martin Ryle, Letter to Carlos Chagas,
Cambridge, 24 February 1983

More and more I come to value charity and love of one's fellow being above everything else... All our lauded technological progress—our very civilization—is like the axe in the hand of the pathological criminal.

—Albert Einstein, Letter to Heinrich Zangger,
Berlin, 6 December 1917

MOKUSATSU

Asked what he'd do first if called upon to rule a nation
Confucius replied, 'I'd correct language.
If language isn't correct
Then what is said is not what's meant
And what ought to be done remains undone.
Morals and art deteriorate
And justice goes astray—
And if justice should disappear
Then people will stand about in helpless confusion.
So there must be no arbitrariness in what's said.
It matters above everything.'

Asked to surrender in World War II
The Japanese used the word *mokusatsu*
In their response to an Allied ultimatum.
The Japanese word meant
'We withhold comment—pending discussion.'
When their reply was sent to Washington
The crucial word was mistranslated,
Its correct meaning being changed for
'We are treating your message with contempt.'
The Americans claimed their ultimatum had been rebuffed
So they were free to play with their new toys.
Two atomic bombs, nicknamed 'Little Boy' and 'Fat Man',
Were then dropped upon Hiroshima and Nagasaki.
A hundred and seventy-five thousand people
Either stood about in helpless confusion
Or were turned into radioactive dust.

Today 'peace' is mistranslated
And means a seething stalemate instead of calm;
'Strength' is mistranslated

I

And means paranoid force instead of right-minded confidence;
'Defence' is mistranslated
And means the compulsive accumulation of profitable weapons
Rather than the thoughtful exercise of skill;
'Testing' is mistranslated
And means the deadly detonation of a nuclear device
Instead of a tentative experiment;
A 'disarmament treaty' is mistranslated
And means junking obsolete weapons because of economic
    restraints
Rather than abandoning technological violence;
'First strike' is mistranslated
And means last strike;
'Security' is mistranslated
And means danger;
'War' is mistranslated—
And we are invited to believe
That war means peace.

FORBIDDEN FRUIT:
OR, THE CYBERNETIC APPLE CORE

Civilization makes hypocrites of us all.
  —Karl Kraus (1874–1936)

Apple last week overtook long-time nemesis Microsoft to become the
world's largest technology company by market value.
  —Reuters, 2 June 2011

As a child, Alan Turing used to bury his broken toys
In the hope that they'd miraculously be mended,
But on digging up a precious train he was upset to find
Wheels were missing and his little bear still eyeless.

In 1922, when Alan was ten, he was given a book,
Natural Wonders Every Child Should Know,
Which, he told his mother, opened his eyes to science;
For in it he read: 'We are made of living bricks.'

'The human body is a Living Apothecary Shop
Where, due to recently discovered hormones,
The different parts of the body are able to signal
To one another with chemical messages.'

The body, this book by Edwin Tenney Brewster
Told Alan, was a machine. 'More complicated
Than any machine ever made with hands; but still
After all a machine.' The book sowed a seed.

When Alan grew older he was intimately drawn
To another boy called Christopher Morcom.
Alan and Chris would sit next to each other in class
And both were passionate mathematicians.

3

When Alan told the maths master he'd 'found the infinite series
For the inverse tangent function',
His teacher, a Mr. Randolph, pronounced Turing to be a genius;
While Alan credited Chris as his muse.

Two shy schoolboys at Sherborne in Dorset
Fell in love for the very first time
With a virginal passion like a bomb in the head
Transforming the fibre of their being.

Alan confessed he 'worshipped the ground Chris trod on'
And that Chris made 'everyone else seem so ordinary'.
The pair plotted comets' paths, then made love in libraries,
Fired-up adolescents snatching electric moments.

Chris engendered feelings in Alan he'd not had before.
Their minds met, then their bodies, then suddenly
Amid their fevered ecstasy Chris died of tuberculosis,
At the age of eighteen. Alan thought he'd die too.

'I shall miss his face so,' Alan wrote to Christopher's mother,
'And the way he used to smile at me sideways.'
Then he told his own mother, 'I feel sure I shall meet Morcom
And there'll be some work for us to do together.'[1]

Unable to let go of Chris or to put his life back together,
Alan found a way of dealing with his grief:
He determined to translate everything he knew of Chris
Into complex scientific constructions.

By his setting down Chris Morcom's likes and dislikes,
Mapping his character with mathematical precision,
And by his customizing a series of algorithmic quanta,
Why couldn't this reunite him with his idol Chris?

When he saw Bernard Shaw's play *Back to Methuselah*,
In which the playwright prophesied that there'd be
No difference between automata and living organisms,
It reinforced Alan's desire to immortalize Chris.

The death of Turing's first love would lead to an obsession
With consciousness, and then with the question
As to whether an ideal machine could have a soul—
Devising ways of resurrecting Chris became a passion.

Chris's mother would write in her diary, after a visit
From Turing's mother, that Alan now believed
That Chris was 'still working with him and helping him'—
Alan meant he was trying to encode his lover.

On visiting Chris's home, the Clock House in Bromsgrove,
He'd sleep in Chris's old sleeping bag.
Convinced Chris was with him in it, he'd then wonder
If the atoms of his friend's brain could be excited

By a non-material spirit 'like a wireless set resonating
To a signal from an unseen world'[2]
And could he recreate a brain that was Chris? He'd say,
'Matter is meaningless in the absence of spirit.'

By building a mathematical periscope to try and peer
Into Chris's absence—his incorporeality—
He believed he could create an artificial intelligence
And thus recreate Chris as an electric effigy.

Alan was destroyed, his great love was gone,
Leaving a huge hole in his mind,
But he nursed the thought of some special way
To contrive the consciousness of his friend.

And he was convinced he was able to achieve this,
Not by visiting spiritual charlatans
For them to fabricate Chris's life in the afterlife—
But by using his and Chris's chosen medium.

Should Alan Turing fail, life wouldn't be worth living
And on seeing *Snow White and the Seven Dwarfs*
Alan would sometimes ponder on Disney's Wicked Witch
Lowering an apple into a cauldron of poison.

5

'*Dip the apple in the brew!*' Alan would sing.
'*Let the Sleeping Death seep through!*'
And in moments of crisis he'd fall back on this rhyme,
As if casting some dark spell upon himself.

Alan went to Cambridge alone, but determined to pursue
'The heroic science of Mathematics',
Which he believed could reduce chaos to order,
And he fielded his idea of an 'electrical brain'—

Something that could solve any problem that was statable
And which, through on-and-off impulses in its circuits,
Could depict anything present in the human nervous system,
Enabling him to render human consciousness computable.

★

Though Alan was an idealist who'd joined anti-war groups
In the hope that war wouldn't break out,
And who'd raised money for striking munitions workers,
When the war began Alan joined up.

Now become a maths don, he was hired by Bletchley Park
Where British Intelligence was desperately trying
To crack the naval codes of the Nazi's Enigma machine
And thus save Allied shipping from U-boat attack.

Thanks to a mechanical breakthrough by Alan Turing,[3]
Enigma's secrets were painstakingly exposed;
Threats from the German submarine fleet were defused
As the Allied navies got to know its every move.

After Turing's ingenuity was credited by Winston Churchill
For winning the war in the North Atlantic,
Turing moved on to envisage mechanizing thought itself
By concentrating on a machine that could learn.

At Manchester University he'd pioneer computing science
Through the universal Turing machine
With which he aimed to store all the information in the world,
Retrieving it from miles and miles of paper tape.

Turing would pave the way for machines that played chess
Through his work on computable numbers[4]
Creating one to win at chess each time—the Turochamp—
But most he hoped for one to store consciousness.

Then when he'd created the field of artificial intelligence
And the basis for the art of programming,
His machine enabled large-scale pulse technology
To turn thoughts into mechanical processes.

This vision that he'd had in 1936 of a machine language
For his universal computing machine
Enabled the creation of the first electronic computer,
The Colossus, whose workings led to the PC.

When he was a boy Turing had designed a typewriter
Which was a machine that manipulated symbols;
Now he foresaw something with its own conscious will
Guided throughout by Chris Morcom, his muse.

When Alan was drunk he'd see Chris; glimpse him
In a fleeting face, hoping to relive his past;
He'd latch on to rent boys who'd trigger a memory,
Then he'd call Chris's name out as he climaxed.

Alan was caught. Arrested, charged, and sentenced
To be forcibly injected with oestrogen
To reduce his libido, then summarily dismissed
From Manchester's research group.

Under British law an offence of 'gross indecency'
Was considered a felony, and to avoid prison
He'd agree to virtual castration by hormone injection.
Thus the country he'd saved would kill him.

On 7 June 1954, Turing's housekeeper found his body,
And nearby was an apple laced with cyanide.
The father of the modern computer had taken a single bite,
Then the poisoned fruit rolled to the floor.

★

In *A Midsummer Night's Dream* the sprightly Puck
Encircles the earth 'in forty minutes'.
Now the dead man's digital progeny surpasses with ease
Puck's feat each fraction of a second.

Likewise Blake would imagine he saw infinity
On contemplating a grain of sand
While chance has it that through slivers of silicon
Turing's infinite mind can set sail.

His infinite mega-brain with computable consciousness
Was created by someone in a wistful dream;
It's a machine with two ghosts in, one called Alan Turing
And another one called Christopher Morcom.

Moreover Alan believed that his thinking machine
Would also be able to feel—
Thus HAL the sad computer in the film *2001*
Was his brainchild, his celluloid heir.

For Alan had once proposed that a test of an intelligent machine
Might be whether or not it was 'influenced by sex appeal'—
Hazarding the conjecture there'd be no artificial intelligence
Without computers having sex drives as well as hard drives,

And when Arthur C. Clarke, *2001*'s science fiction author,
Revealed that HAL was modelled on Alan Turing
Clarke was soon asked if the feline-voiced HAL was gay
But he discreetly replied that he'd 'never asked him'.

Not only HAL, but Silicon Valley and indeed the whole IT world
Would grow out of the fumblings of two schoolboys.
For Chris and Alan's exchanging a kiss would change everything,
While other boys played football oblivious.

On looking for a logo for a computer company in the US
A bright PR spark would propose an apple:
For while signalling innocence, plus Newton and the Beatles,
What'd give it extra gravitas would be Turing.

It's rumoured Apple's apple is a homage to his memory—
A slyly insensitive reference to his suicide—
If not a macabre joke shared by the geeks at Apple
In California to whom it's part of their history.[5]

On visiting their headquarters in Cupertino, Silicon Valley,
You can buy slick goods bearing the emblem:
T-shirts with a bitten apple and punning captions
Such as 'Byte into an Apple'—'Bite' with a 'y'.

Thousand of miles away in Shenzhen and Chengdu,
Apple's silver and snow-white computers
Are churned out in millions with revenues in billions
And each gadget displays the glowing logo.

Four hundred thousand men and women working twelve-hour days
Are called upon to assemble Apple products
And for serving Apple's manufacturer, Foxconn,
An Apple worker gets a daily wage of £5.20.

Ironically forbidden to speak while they assemble
Devices designed to facilitate communication,
Apple workers have anti-suicide nets outside their windows
Owing to a virus infecting their industrial relations:

In May 2010 seven Chinese workers producing Apple iPads
Formed a cluster of suicides among Apple's workforce—
Made to pay for food and lodging from a paltry 65p an hour
A note said, 'We are treated inhumanely, like machines.'

Yet a little blood on a keyboard or on some circuitry
Is of no concern provided it dries out,
Workers live or die but not corporate super-entities:
They'll cling to life whatever the cost.[6]

Relatives of those whom cybernetics has driven to suicide
Hold up placards outside the Apple stores
In which a voracious maggot peers out from Apple's logo.
Floating on blood, it's captioned 'Bloody Apple'.[7]

The mourners' loved ones are now dead, and no avatars,
No iPads, no iPhones, no iPods, no Macbooks
Can replace flesh and blood or reboot them back to life.
They're broken, like Alan Turing's buried toys.

'Golly golly wow wow! Seen the latest killer apps?
Thunderbolt connection. Awesome download speed.
Solid-state hard drive. I swear to God this tablet rocks—
Chips that can memorize the whole freakin' world.'

In June 2011 a seventeen-year-old student called Zheng
In the eastern Anhui Province
Sold his kidney to buy an iPad and got 22,000 yuan,
Or $3,393, and a long red scar.

After the operation was performed at Chenzhou Hospital,
Zheng then developed serious health problems,
Though now cybernetic consumerism links man to machine
He may draw comfort from being a true cyborg.[8]

★

Machines mimic thought but not conscience.
Computers depend on coltan for memory,
A blood mineral mined in the Congo by child labourers
Who die for a machine invented to deal with grief.

The apple in the Garden of Eden was a forbidden fruit
And, in that Bronze Age fable, a disembodied voice
Told man that by acquiring knowledge he'd forfeit Eden—
An illusory Eden equally elusive as techno-paradise.

According to Glyn Hughes, who's sculpted a Turing memorial,
Which has him sat on a park bench holding a bronze apple,
An Apple computer was buried below the founder of cyberspace
As an indication of what Turing had died for.

On a visit to this statue in Sackville Park, Manchester,
To see the man whom Andrew Hodges describes
As a 'non-violent Nelson saving democracy from fascism'
Alan Turing's park was quiet and he was seated alone—

There was no one there save an exuberant sheepdog
Racing around the stationary figure;
It'd stop to look up at Turing's statue expectantly
As if believing he could throw it a stick.

Worldwide Alan Turing is undervalued or forgotten
Compared with the Apple corporation—
The world's largest technology company making billions
By turning people into its supercult's consumers.

Notes

1. Such direct speech is taken from Andrew Hodges, *Alan Turing: The Enigma*, London, Burnett Books, 1983.

2. Ibid., p. 63.

3. 'In 1939–40 Alan Turing and another Cambridge mathematician, Gordon Welchman, designed a new machine, the British Bombe. The basic property of the Bombe was that it could break any Enigma-enciphered message, provided that the hardware of the Enigma was known and that a plaintext "crib" of about 20 letters could be guessed accurately.'
   www.turing.org.uk/turing/scrapbook/ww2.html.

4. 'On computable numbers, with an application to the *Entscheidungsproblem*', *Proc. Lond. Math. Soc.* (2), 42 (1937).

5. 'While I was attending the 2002 Edinburgh International Festivals in Scotland, a lecturer made the statement that the famous Apple Computer logo (a profile of a rainbow colored apple with a bite out of it) was in homage to Alan Turing, the generally acknowledged father of the computer and the developer of the "Turing Test", which pioneered the field of artificial intelligence.' Greg Gore, 'Understanding the enigma of the Apple Computer logo', *Daily Local News*, West Chester, PA, 12 February, 2003. Another reference linking the Apple Computer logo with Turing's suicide can be found at:
   www.fusionanomaly.net/alanturing.html.

6. 'Apple's Steve Jobs finds Foxconn deaths "troubling".' Reuters, 1 June 2010.

7. Gethin Chamerlain, 'Inside the iSweat shops: Apple factories accused of exploiting Chinese workers', *Observer*, 1 February 2011, p. 5.

8. Martin Patience, 'China teenager sells kidney for iPad', BBC News, Beijing, 3 June 2011.

What if the Sun in the sky were self-conscious?
A wide-awake being suspended in space...?
Gaia theory says that the Earth's self-regulation
Means Earth, the Sun's offspring, has a mind.

Therefore Earth's original parent has to be aware too
As it mindfully guides the Solar System;
Or is this potent Sun, once adored as a celestial god,
Just an object, inanimate and unthinking?

Yet it's a 'something' still prayed to by worshippers:
'Please may it be sunny tomorrow,
Then everyone'll feel good and we'll enjoy ourselves,
So don't burn out and come to an end.'

'I'm going to soak up the sun,
While it's still free
I'm going to soak up the sun
Before it goes out on me.'[1]

The pervasive presence of a huge golden sphere
Is the most glaring fact of man's existence.
Nothing happens without the Sun's supervision—
Everything's in its light or in its shadow.

Every gamma-ray in the Sun's core is converted
Into billions of photons of visible light
Taking 30,000 years to reach its surface
Before they escape to light up the world.

The Sun's a star made of seething hot plasma
Interwoven with vast magnetic fields.
The Sun in the sky is over a million times
The size of the Earth, its tiny protégé—

It's a nuclear fireball permanently exploding
Whose dragon-like flares can interact
With Earth's magnetic field and create auroras
To silence satellite chatter in a flash.

If it was personified what might it be like? *'Looking at me?*
I'm solid charisma and I'll blind you!
I've brain cells of fiery gas the size of planets,
And when I stop thinking, you'll die!'

Yet, when it rises, it dispels inner and outer darkness
Like a shaman performing a mass healing:
Its rays dissolve misery and its dawns can endow
Every life form with a fresh beginning.

'Here Comes the Sun', Beatles.
'Turn Up the Sun', Oasis.
'Sunshine Daydream', Grateful Dead.
'Holidays in the Sun', Sex Pistols.

Ruskin declared sunshine to be 'delicious'.
Someone else has said that to be loved
And to love feel the same as having warm sun
On your back and your front both at once.

'Let the sun saturate me with love.
The only place I wanna be.
Let the sun shine down on me.'
Sang the Kinks in 'Lavender Hill'.

And to surf naked in the sun is to be mythical—
Mermaids and mermen balancing on water;
Shape-shifting, levitating, riding high on tall crests
While a glowing eye looks down from above.

'Here comes the sun!'—An enormous entity
Desalinates seawater to make rain
Then grows generations of sunshine supermen
On the third stone along from a seminal star—

The unavoidably exuberant, all-surpassing Sun
Whose every photon tells you
You've been caught up in a solar spin-cycle
Whether you're aware of it or not.

Sunlight hits the eye, the brain, and the pineal gland
Where it manufactures serotonin,
The fuel of consciousness that gives the soul a spurt
To help it make sense of life, or not.

And the body the Sun made for you outlasts you
Since your particles, your DNA dust,
Will float in its sunbeams and rainbows forever,
Whether you relish sunshine or not.

At the solstice, the Sun models for man's study
By momentarily standing still—
This transcendent ball is floating through space
Then pauses as it changes direction.

The Sun, *sol* in Latin, has a stoppage,
It has a *stitium*—*solstitium*—or solstice,
Meaning the Sun comes to a significant halt
And the nearby world can reflect on it—

Seeing its democratic glow shine into cesspits
While remaining uncontaminated itself;
Seeing with relief it's out of oil markets' reach,
While its solar energy is going for free.

At its core, the Sun fuses 600 million metric tons
Of hydrogen particles every second
Which, as they change into helium, release photons
And the Sun's energy is barely tapped.

The Sun detonates a trillion-megaton bomb each second
Making Earth's nuclear plants a sick joke—
For the world's total power requirement is 20 terawatts
Yet solar radiance hands it a hundred thousand.

Thus having sparked off civilization, this mega-power
That's initiated every first and last life form
Lavishes Earth with the means by which to sustain itself
Once man has worked out how to harness it.

And a tree's solar cells are perfect transformers,
Its branches echoing the Fibonacci scale,
So all that's required to collect sunlight efficiently
Is simply to imitate nature's own methods.

Size isn't everything but if the Sun outsizes this planet
By a factor of over a million
And if the Sun's survived for 4.5 billion years
It's unlikely to be totally dim.

The ancient Egyptian *Book of the Dead* describes
How a spiritual being called Ra incarnated
As a bright solar disc with radiant haloes of flame
To bring warmth to a cold sea of darkness.

As man's arrival here is due to sunshine it makes sense
To ask, since man can think, whether man's matrix
Might not also be self-willed—mightn't have a purpose,
While the Sun's ingeniously turning matter into light.

Clusters of subatomic particles triggered by shock waves
From nearby supernovae formed this glittering star
Of huge hydrogen clouds collapsing on top of themselves
And making a cosmic compost sparkling with light.

Shafts of sunlight would then stream down to Earth
And its lifeless primordial soup
To ignite its chemicals and change them into protein—
The very first building blocks of life.

The Sun's light transformed earthly gas into breathable air;
Light that can sweeten plants till they're food—
Thus, on the crusty surface of a planet brimful of magma,
Human fire-walkers can live by biting the Sun.

And through this powerful god, in all but name, that's created
Every living thing in the world—
And with Mercury, symbolizing immortality, dancing round it—
Man can vote daily for happiness.

For the Sun's a space doctor practising distant healing
With its rays that strengthen our immunity;
Stimulating the blood's circulation and the endorphins—
The hormones that magically chase off pain.

'When the Sun shines, we'll shine together,' people exclaim.
'Let the Sun wrap its arms around me.'
On bright mornings people smile as if they're connected
By an irresistible current and become what they see.

Soaking up doctor Sun's light synthesizes vitamin D,
Which makes possible the absorption of calcium
For organisms to grow bones, though lesser gods prefer
To dispatch their fans to break bones with bullets.

There are no priests or hierarchies in a solar religion
And no one's discriminated against;
The Sun shines on everyone and its worship requires
No weird beliefs or annual donations.

No one's at war over the Sun despite its being priceless
And as gods go it may be hard to do better
For temples and churches can be as cold as any grave,
While communing with the Sun warms the soul.

The Sun qualifies as a god by being unapproachable;
It's untouchable and it's still unexplained:
No scientist orbiting round it can say why it's there
Nor what it's doing by compulsively shining;

Nor why the Sun also sings—for its core emits signals
Whereby looped magnetic fields are plucked;
Surface oscillations are heard to boom like a pipe organ,
Hinting the Sun may beat time with the Universe.

Although it's sung and shone for 4.5 billion years
It's fated to expand into a red giant;
A new entity that'll overwhelm the entire planet Earth
And cause seas to evaporate with a hiss—

An enveloping giant, once benign, will eat this earthly nugget
With those on its surface vanishing with hardly a trace
As the Solar System fades and its ghosts are left to swirl in the dark,
Each wistfully sighing, 'Make hay while the Sun shines.'

Notes

1. Sheryl Crow, 'Soak Up the Sun'.

BEING KEPT BY A JACKDAW

At a country fair a couple called Dave and Di Nelstrop
Came from Bow, in Devon, to sell tansy pancakes—
Bringing skillets, a brazier, a mound of flour and eggs,
They drew customers to their tent by the good smell.

Behind a striped awning there was a stack of wooden cages
Which they'd carried with them, each with an injured bird.
One was a large crow, a raven, they referred to as Aubrey;
His door was left open and he caught me in his glare.

Between bites washed down with a blue mug of sweet tea
I began confessing to something I'd always yearned for.
'Ever since childhood...' They looked patiently quizzical,
'I've wanted...' I paused again, transfixed by the crow—

Hopping on black legs, scanning me with a needle eye,
Black as those Victorian jet stones from Whitby,
He'd expose a scarlet throat and then he'd caw in my face
With a sound as old as Egypt that said, 'I know you—

'I've pecked your ancestors' bones and nibbled your DNA
And I'll penetrate your soul with my carrion cries.'
Aubrey's eerie presence triggered an old boyhood dream
Of having a jackdaw on your shoulder, like a pirate.

Whispering secrets in your ear, this jackdaw would speak
In a language that only you could understand.
You and the jackdaw. You and this bird. A medieval bond
Like young Arthur's falcon trained by Merlin.

Only a jackdaw would be much more worldly wise,
Independent, and even faintly criminal.
Lifting jewels from open windows if you were broke;
Teaching you things no one else knew.

19

As I watched Aubrey retire to his cage, demanding food
And a cloth draped on top so he could sleep,
Dusk settled and Aubrey fell silent; then I blurted it out,
'I've always wanted to look after a jackdaw.'

Dave Nelstrop said casually, 'Oh, we've got one.
A fledgling. It was too poorly to bring.
It's being fed by a dripper. With touches of brandy.
It just fell out of its nest in a bell-tower.'

They promised to bring it when next they were passing.
'Does it have a name?' I asked when they arrived.
'Could call it Jack,' Dave suggested. 'Surname of Daw.'
He grinned. 'Until something else better occurs.'

But 'Jack Daw' seemed workman-like and so it stuck.
Then I stared, bewildered by this quaint creature:
Once childishly romanticized, it was radically different
From the parrot on Long John Silver's tricorn hat.

At close quarters its feral behaviour was dominated
By a consuming curiosity, but who was it exactly?
This bird that had lived its life in a tower, then fallen,
And whose cowl made it look like a hooded monk.

It would wake at dawn and shadow me till dusk.
We'd find mealworms, then warm up some milk.
The one fact it knew was that in order to survive
I'd have to be converted into its servile minion.

So Jack behaved like some tyrannical movie star,
Demanding full attention day and night
With a vampire's knack of spotting the submissive,
Then getting them to run endless errands.

Almost immediately I became the bird's captive,
Existing solely to attend to its needs,
Wondering if I'd experience Stockholm Syndrome,
Which means you fall in love with your captors.

But this bonsai pterodactyl was quite hard to love—
A dive-bombing comet of energy and appetite.
At daybreak its beak was pushed between my lips,
Searching for a morsel from last night's meal.

A bony road-drill picking at your teeth was how Jack
Alerted you to the unpalatable fact
That instead of being an independent human being
You were now mobile carrion ruled by a bird.

My body clock was retuned to keep jackdaw hours:
To wake at dawn, then to feel tired at dusk.
It was unsettling to fall asleep as soon as it got dark
And realize how electricity had made you a moth.

Yet there were long days of elation: digging up a patch
With a jackdaw perched on your head;
Keeping watch from its new tower and swooping down
To display its skills as a metal detector.

Buried bottle tops would be brought to the surface,
Along with fragments of bright silver foil,
Invoking the ghosts of picnics past, then sixpences
Were teased out and offered as treasure trove.

'He's trading you level,' an old countryman said,
Stopping by to watch such transactions.
'You give him food and shelter. He gives you coin.
What you'd call satisfaction all round.'

When the philosopher Thoreau was hoeing his garden
A young sparrow alighted on his shoulder;
Thoreau said he felt 'more distinguished by that event
Than by an epaulet'. I knew what he meant.

Another visitor, Bernie Skuse, a poacher from Bristol,
Said, 'Tell you what we used to do, boy.
Sharpen the edge of a coin and set it under his tongue.
Cuts through the tendon, then he'll talk.'

I thanked Bernie but said I wasn't sure that I wanted
To torture Jack into speaking my language—
I guessed he'd just tell me what I'd taught him to say,
And I imagined he had thoughts of his own.

Bird-like thoughts. From a miniature mind, aeons old,
That had evolved feathers and grown them from skin.
Initially earthbound, it had had Icarus' dream of flying,
Flinging itself higher and higher till it stayed aloft.

I'd now also dream nightly I had wings on my shoulders,
I steered with the feathers sprouting from my heels.
And I'd wonder, since I woke feeling a firm ally of this elf,
If he could have been the projectionist of such flights.

Then gradually I suspected that he was preparing to go.
Being mended, the fierce bond that he'd made
First with the Nelstrops, his rescuers, and later with myself
Was now weakening at the sight of other birds.

Each evening there were flocks of rooks and jackdaws
Passing overhead on their way to the estuary.
Jack looked up at them and gave a quietly uncertain cry
Belonging neither to one world nor the other.

Each day was spent on my shoulder and each day
He'd fly off, and would always come back—
He flew in circles but they'd increase in diameter
As the time would come for him never to return.

I'd look up at the sky, studying tree after tree,
And ask people if they'd seen a jackdaw.
'Pinch something of yours? That's what they do.'
And I would realize that in a way he had.

When seeing a clattering of jackdaws—the collective noun
For these gregarious birds that pair-bond for life—
I'd be more alerted by their gatherings than by anything else:
The jackdaw tribe's peripatetic parliaments.

Spread across fields, seething carpets of glistening flecks—
I'd scrutinize each jackdaw in turn.
Watch them scavenging a sheep's carcass on the hillside
Hoping to jog one avian memory.

A judgemental friend said, 'You shouldn't have tamed it.
You've put its life in peril. I heard of someone
Took a bird in, then, when they released it, it was so tame
It landed on the barrel of a sportsman's gun.

'Got itself blown to bits, didn't it?' I became troubled.
I hadn't tamed it, but undeterred they finished off
Their unsolicited obituary with, 'Just a bird, wasn't it?'
I then buried myself in folklore, it being less brutal.

To country science nothing's 'just a bird' but can foretell rain
Or death, when jackdaws nest in a chimney.
A jackdaw can signify a birth whenever seen on the rooftop;
Each movement in nature is meant to be read.

'The quick brown fox jumps over the lazy dog'
Contains all the letters of the alphabet,
As does 'Jackdaws love my big sphinx of quartz',
Yet no arrangement of the letters solves the riddle—

The riddle that I was left with, far harder to resolve
Than the age-old riddle of the Sphinx:
'What goes on four legs in the morning, two at noon,
And on three legs at evening time?'

The answer being man himself, who crawls first on four,
Then stands on two, then on three counting his stick—
But the impossible riddle the jackdaw had posed was why
Man has determined to end his life with no legs at all.

Yet while civilization proves to be of questionable value
In helping him to find his niche in the universe,
A jackdaw can behave as if completely assured of its place
And with a comic beauty that's close to perfection.

Someone told me that Hermann, Kafka's father, had a sign
In front of the family's fancy goods shop in Prague.
It was a painting of a jackdaw set above their trade name—
For *kavka* means 'jackdaw' in Czech.

I discovered Kafka had always identified with his namesake:
He described a jackdaw kept by the coal merchant
Near Tein Cathedral as 'my relative', saying he sympathized
With its longing 'to disappear between the stones'.

Kafka told the young poet Gustav Janouch,
'We find relations with animals easier than with men.'
Adding that, 'Animals are closer to us than human beings.'
The coal merchant's jackdaw struck a chord.

Unsurprisingly—for birds are the uncredited inventors
Of music, and all of them continue singing for joy:
Cost-free, unlike man's derivative warblings for profit.
'I hope you love birds too?' Emily Dickinson asked.

'It is economical. It saves going to heaven.' I do. It is. It does.
I still see that questing figure; I pick up on his cries.
The *tchack tchack*, eight times. And the eyes, the pale blue iris
And the intense pupils studying things miles away.

Jack Daw. A foot long. Black, shot with steel blue. Grey nape.
Demonically sprightly. Bustling and strutting.
Jerkily swaggering, then pausing to shuffle along the ground
As he turns everything over, clods and stones—

Searching for something reflective to present with a flourish
While ripping up rival possessions, like books, into shreds.
'Anyone,' Kafka said, 'who keeps the ability to see beauty
Never grows old.' A jackdaw's hop puts a skip in my step.

DARWIN'S NOSE

Everything existing in the universe is the fruit of chance and necessity.
  —Democritus (*fl.* 5th century BC)

Evolution might never have been sniffed out
Because of the shape of Darwin's nose,
Thanks to which its owner was almost rejected
For the position of naturalist on board the *Beagle*.

The ship's captain, Robert Fitzroy,
Was a disciple of Lavater, who believed
You could judge people's character by their looks,
And Fitzroy doubted, in Darwin's words, that

'Anyone with my nose could possess
Sufficient energy and determination for the voyage.
But I think he was afterwards well satisfied
That my nose had spoken falsely.'

When Pascal considered Cleopatra's large nose,
Wondering what if it had been an inch shorter,
He decided that: 'The whole face of the world
Would have been changed beyond recognition.'

The size of the Queen's nose gave her confidence
And this, Pascal thought, paved the way
For her to nose her way blithely into Caesar's bed
And screw up the entire Roman Empire.

Likewise Darwin could screw the Creationists,
Snorting at their fundamentalist beliefs.
Man's secondary sexual characteristic told him
There was a world before Adam smelt it.

THE ATOMIC MUSEUM

Hiroshima bomb earrings for sale.
  —Independent, 6 August 1999

In the National Atomic Museum
At Albuquerque, New Mexico,
You can buy souvenirs of 'Little Boy',
The bomb that demolished Hiroshima,
And of 'Fat Man', named after the bomb
That destroyed Nagasaki three days later.

They come from what the museum
Calls its 'Exclusive' collection:
'Little Boy' earrings in sterling silver
Cost twenty-four dollars for the pair;
And 'Fat Man', the counter clerk says,
'Comes in at thirty dollars' as
'More precious metal is used.'

'They're a great seller,' says the museum storekeeper,
Mike Romero, who assures enquirers,
'We don't hold political opinions.
We only present the facts.
If you go to a zoo you can buy a stuffed elephant.
We are the only atomic museum in the US
So we have to sell related merchandise.
I don't think it's tasteless. It was before my time
And it doesn't strike at my heart at all.'

But the fact that these atomic 'facts'
(Namely everything being obliterated
Within a three-mile radius of the bombs)

Doesn't strike at his heart at all
Evokes D.H. Lawrence's unforgiving view:
'The essential American soul is hard, isolate, stoic, and a killer.
It has never yet melted'—
This was written when Lawrence was living in New Mexico,
In a place that would later become the bomb's birthplace;
It was where an Imperial power's big stick
Would be tried out on the Alamogordo test range—
A bomb designed to whack a rival power with mega-deaths.

The knick-knacks and novelties in the Atomic Museum
Commemorate, in souvenir form,
The vaporizing of two Japanese cities.
Somehow this, and the ensuing distortions of man's DNA
Followed by the bomb's contagion of unnatural sickness,
Is thought to be worth celebrating with a national memorial—
Albeit that the bomb was superfluous to requirements,
Since the Japanese had been seeking an honourable surrender.

However, US militarists, eager to stretch the war into World War III,
Used the bomb to demonstrate to their Russian rivals
Who was the alpha male and which of their mutually misguided
    boffins
Was the best—'USA! USA!'—So, bang went 'Little Boy',
And bang went 'Fat Man', and these patriotic bangs were followed
By excruciating suffering and cancerous pandemics
And radioactive waves of paranoia that lasted for decades:
Despite perpetual poison clouds hovering overhead
Each one of them containing a madman's thought bubble
Boasting that life on earth could be ended forever.
And despite the US having bomb-casing arsenals in 27 countries
With the plutonium charges needed to render them nuclear
Hidden in 27 embassies, threatening a hundred holocausts.
It would prove a boon one day to the souvenir market.
The bomb that was an irrational Empire's bargaining chip
In an unwinnable war game was forged here,
And novelty knick-knacks are now produced to prove it.

The Atomic Museum was established by Congressional Charter
To indicate the pride the Empire took in its deadly heritage
Though, when the UK journalist James Cameron
Witnessed an early atomic test on Bikini Atoll,
Which would turn the surrounding seas into a sickly desert,
He said he thought he could hear a door slam in hell.
All this is now lovingly commemorated in the museum
With 'Authentic bomb blast goggles, as used in the Pacific
During nuclear testing' being available for purchase.

The museum's entrance is guarded by phalanxes of missiles
Pointing, like admonitory fingers: '*Be afraid. Be very afraid.*'
Four California girls drift round the museum's Heritage Park.
They paw at the bombs, and stroke the undercarriage of a B-29,
Then emerge, giggling, from a mocked-up atomic shelter
To enter an area set aside by the museum for more 'Fun Stuff'
And sprawl over its showcases sizing up the goods on offer.

A 'Little Boy' wine cork and a 'Fat Man' shot glass;
Posters of mushroom clouds with palm trees in the foreground;
Knick-knacks decorated with bombers and their waving crews;
Reprints of the *Daily News*, 'ATOM BOMB ROCKS JAPS';
A 'Get a Half-Life' mug for your favourite beverage;
Atomic hatpins, atomic tie-clips, and nuclear golf balls.
The museum once even had a line in Atomic Bomb perfume,
Which reputedly smelled like the end of the world.

The laid-back visitors spot the Atomic Museum's jewellery—
Miniature versions of the huge bombs they just strolled past,
Lying around the Heritage Park like bloated gravestones.
'Hey, guys. Cute!' one says, poring over the showcases,
'Yeah, gotta have them, dude. You think they come in gold?'
'What about platinum? Platinum would be dead cool.'

For a split second, the word sounds like 'plutonium'—
'Plutonium would be dead cool,' one seems to have said.
Then, with a numb laconic smile, as if embodying death itself,
The clerk slides the triumphalist trophies and trinkets
Across the counter to satisfy their short attention spans.

All four then sidle out of the shop in the Atomic Museum
With their bang-bang bling now dangling from their ears
For Cameron to hear another door slam in hell
As, returning from one more mission to make fear-mongering fun,
The devil now concentrates on the prototype of his Zyklon B
    paperweight,
To buff up his '*Arbeit Macht Frei*' keyrings, and more Death's
    Head kitsch,
And to tweak his software upgrade of Nazi Playstation 3.

Then he chuckles, recalling Mary Meyer,[1] the Washington hostess
Who turned Kennedy on to marijuana for dreamier sex;
She'd joke with him in a White House bedroom about their both
    being high
When the time came for her presidential lover
To press the nuclear button and blow the world to smithereens . . .

Whereupon the devil picks out a roach end and a condom,
And he covers them in gold leaf before he gives them pride of place
In the gleaming showcases of the Atomic Museum.

Notes

1. Ian Brodie, 'Kennedy's love link with the Mafia is dead,' *The
    Times*, 27 September 1999.

THE FIRST PHOTOGRAPH EVER TAKEN
OF A HUMAN BEING

The first photograph ever taken of a human being
Was of a bootblack kneeling down in front of his client
In Paris, in the Boulevard du Temple, in 1838.

Louis-Jacques-Mandé Daguerre took the photograph
On a fifteen-minute exposure. The man whose footwear
Is being attended to is wearing a long tailcoat

And looks like a proudly plutocratic beetle.
By contrast, the bootblack, bent double in a servile posture,
Is obscured, hidden by a perpendicular pile of smudges.

His figure can barely be discerned, as he squats on the ground
With his equipment laid out beside him; a leafless sapling
Sprouting out of a tall blackened cage rises up behind him.

As the picture of the tree-lined boulevard has no depth of field,
This caged urban shrub seems to emerge directly from his head
As if he himself was the bed in which the plant had been rooted.

Then you decipher more clearly how he's placed: head bowed—
A rough hint of a hand as it scrapes, brushes and polishes
A haughtily proffered boot at the end of a languorous leg.

But although he's the only person doing anything,
Somehow he's marginalized and his presence belittled
By the position which fate has forced him to adopt.

Yet he's a man at work—trying to make a stranger look good—
But whose destiny is to have these chance shapes define his
  existence
And for them to be all that the world may ever know of him.

*

When the images of these two people were captured
Slavery still existed in the United States.
Frederick Douglass would escape from it in that year.

Germany did not exist; nor was there an Italy.
The steam locomotive was the sole form of mechanized transport,
And the distance to the nearest star had only just been calculated.

Another world. But, judging by how man has conducted himself
In the interim and by all the dubious poses that he has struck
In the course of revealing himself to history's watchful eye,

The last photograph of a human being ever to be taken
Will echo this one, even reflecting Orwell's image of the future:
'A boot stamping on a human face—forever.'

Nearly two centuries later, after Daguerre had snapped
These two anonymous celebrities, man's situation is the same:
Dominant parties pressurize others into subservience

Forcing them to be anxious to please; to humiliate themselves
For the sake of a crust of bread, or for some paltry recompense,
Or for a roof, on the condition that others are able to exploit
   them

And steal away their lives with the rapacity of locusts—
Flinging them a couple of coins by way of remuneration.
Not unexpectedly it leads to the rise of intractable tensions

Between those who don't clean their own shoes and who own
   things
And the people whom they pay to do so and who own nothing.
It causes insoluble resentment that builds up into huge
   explosions

And then into the charred and blackened ruins which the final
   shutter-click
On the last human being will inevitably convey—
A freeze-frame recording the same divisions as the first.

★

Though man's been photographing himself for nearly two
    centuries
He still can't see the light despite a 200-year exposure
In a darkroom of his own making; addicted to his own image

Of which this fragile figure, suggesting the Tin Man, was the
    first example:
This surreal cyborg with a chimney-brain, but in whose lines
    coincidentally
There's the ideogram for water: indestructible, like the
    bootblack's photons.

CCTV

Walking through London
You'll be caught on camera
Some 300 times.

Big Brother's robots
Will follow your every move.
Star on State TV!

Do you know yourself?
Other people think that they
Know all about you.

Solely by sticking
Their electronic noses
Into your business.

Banks of cameras
Are logging all your movements:
'Here, follow that one.'

Invisible sneaks
And electronic telltales
Exchange your data:

Secretive software
Sells your profile for profit
To security

Or market research,
Mapping your behaviour
'Twenty-four seven'—

Forcing money's rule
Over the regulated
Lab-rats in their maze:

Don't step out of line,
Interfere with the traffic,
Or look suspicious—

Uniformed goblins
Will appear out of nowhere
And freeze-frame your life.

Yet you can subvert
All this high-tech surveillance
With a low-tech mask.

Real terrorists,
In any case, hide behind
Banks and governments.

BEES

Wise bees will tell you:
'*Natura in minima
Maxima*'—kindly

Translating it
As 'Nature is the greatest
In the smallest things.'

Bees' making life sweet
Made man's harsh evolution
More tolerable.

Almost each mouthful
Of food owes its existence to
Pollinating bees.

It's been said, 'If bees
Disappear, man has only
A few years to live.'

Bees are eusocial—
Meaning their life is ordered
For the benefit

Of everyone in
The hive: construction workers,
Nurses, guards, grocers,

Its housekeepers and
Foragers, and gigolos
And undertakers.

Man's society
Is largely antisocial—
A kleptocracy.

We, who steal from bees,
Repay them with pesticide;
Yet they dance to work.

Emma Goldman said
That all revolutions should
Involve dancing, but

No revolution
Has produced anything
As good as bees

And Tolstoy believed
Their ideal society
Could enlighten man.

No society
Has a talisman with the
Power of honey.

One ounce of honey
Enables a bee to fly
Round the whole world.

If bees' stamina
Is scaled up to human level,
Man is quite outclassed.

A bee beats its wings
Over eleven thousand
Times in a minute.

Its brain's a cubic
Millimetre whose wiring
Beats silicon chips.

A bee, said Karl Marx,
Can 'put architects to shame
In constructing cells'.

The bee's venom is
The most powerful substance
In the natural world.

Bee acupuncture
Can extend man's lifespan by
Curing arthritis.

A bee's venom can
Open up neural pathways
Following a stroke.

Honey can dress wounds—
Since microbes can't live in it,
It's antiseptic.

Alexander the
Great was embalmed in honey
And lasted decades.

In Ephesus, bees
Would symbolize Artemis,
And stood for wisdom.

So Pythagoras
And Plato were fed honey
In their infancy.

The 'gift of heaven'
Virgil called it and,
In his *Georgics*,

He said it conveyed
Prescience; and the priestess
At Delphi was called

The 'Delphic Bee' as
Her powers were oracular:
She saw the future.

Before Chernobyl
Was understood, bees wisely
Would stay in their hives.

The priest Jonathan,
In 1 *Samuel* 14:25,
Would take some honey

From a honeycomb
Then, 'as his hand met his mouth,
His eyes were enlightened.'

The letters in the
Poet Deborah's Hebrew name,
DBR, mean bee;

It also means truth—
Both being on a mission
To improve the world

With sweetness and light.
For if reason's sweet
Why pull a sour face?

Bees have made honey
For 150 million years
And the Pyramids,

When rediscovered,
Showed that honey had been placed
Near Pharaoh's body—

An immortal food
Which still tasted good after
Five thousand years.

Bees defend themselves
Without paying someone else
To do it for them.

Bees' flower power
Is not a drug-enhanced dream:
Their flying's for real.

'Where the bee sucks, there
Suck I, in a cowslip's bell
I lie.' *Paradise!*

The buzzing of bees,
Indicating contentment,
Is archetypal—

The soundtrack to the
Land of milk and honey, man's
Sustaining ideal.

Inner consciousness
In Sanskrit is *brahmari*:
The buzzing of bees.

Their sound while they drink
From flowers eases tension.
You're at one with life.

Each bee has five eyes.
Mystics reckon a third eye
Bestows occult powers.

Five eyes might give you
The ability to see
Some things that man can't.

Beekeepers often
'Tell the bees' if, let's say, death
Has struck their family.

What the bees tell us
Is being overlooked since
We think we own them.

EINSTEIN ON A BIKE

When the *Titanic*
Sailed into New York harbour
Time-travellers cheered.

The booking office
Of Marie Celeste Travel
Opened for business.

The missing Shergar
Came back from the dead and then
Won the National

Just as the tipster
Prince Monolulu foretold.
Time's a bicycle.

Albert Einstein thought
Up the Special Theory of
Relativity

While riding his bike.
'Bicycle cyborgs
Are man's future,'

He said in 2020,
'Unless you wish to go back
To the Dark Ages.'

He also said: 'Life
Is like riding a bicycle:
To keep your balance

You must keep moving.'
And fellow visionary
H. G. Wells pronounced

That 'Cycle tracks will
Abound in Utopia.
Every time I see

'Someone on a bike
I no longer despair of
The human race.

'Who can there be left
Who won't see it's the machine
For the Earth's future?'

And the Grateful Dead
Said they're 'better than guitars
For picking up girls'.

Bicycles go forward
Without wasting anything,
Suiting runaway hearts.

The bicycle wheel
Turns the clock back in time with
A perfect machine.

THE TIGERS OF WRATH

Without the breath of the tiger there will be no wind, only clouds, and certainly no rain.
  —I Ching (*c*.1000 BC)

Currently, a poached tiger is believed to fetch between $25,000 and $50,000 for the carcass, penis and bones. Largely as a result of this lucrative, illegal trade, there are estimated to be only 3,200 tigers left in the wild—down from 100,000 a century ago.
  —Guardian, 24 November 2010

Before William Blake wrote his poem 'The Tyger',
He'd paid several visits to the Tower of London
Where three tigers were permanently confined
In England's gloomiest state prison.

Blake would imagine the tigers behind their bars
'Burning bright in the forests of the night',
When from Lambeth he'd hear their unhappy sounds,
Roaring and snarling and growling.

Then he saw them, pacing the cage which enclosed them,
These newly trafficked arrivals, *Panthera tigris*—
Each a prisoner in the British Empire's oldest death camp,
Where human threats to the State were decapitated.

Blake would study what the naturalist Linnaeus had called
'The most beautiful of all wild creatures'.
Their keeper casually accepted stray dogs as an admission fee.
Blake preferred to pay the standard threepence.

The tiger family had been given mildly humorous names:
Will and Phyllis and their son Dick;
But it was the animals' anger that Blake noticed most of all
And he'd liken it to revolutionary frenzy.

43

He thought the tiger embodied 'the fierce forces in the soul
Needed to break the bonds of experience'—
And he'd imagine the tigers' stripes as impassioned flames
Lighting up something fresh in his understanding.

'In what clay,' Blake asked, in an early draft of the poem,
'And in what mould, were thy eyes of fury rolled?'
He asked this as the British establishment trembled
At the thought of France's revolution spreading.

As Tory MPs railed, in their words, against a 'republic of tigers'
Which they saw gathering strength across the Channel.
One likened the eyes of Jean-Paul Marat to a 'tiger cat's'
And others recoiled from a revolutionary 'tribunal of tigers'.

But while Parliament decried the French uprising as 'bestial',
The London street was viewing it quite differently:
'The time is come you plainly see,' ran a rhyme of the 1790s,
'The government opposed must be.'

So, after relating to the 'wild furies from the tiger's brain',
Blake wrote a valentine to this primeval terrorist
Coming from regions of uncontrolled instinct, now confined,
But who spoke to him of unfathomable desires.

'What immortal hand or eye could frame
Thy fearful symmetry?' Blake asks the tiger,
As he carefully etched the tiger's flickering camouflage
That helped it move invisibly through long grasses.

'In what distant deeps or skies,' he queried,
'Burnt the fire of thine eyes?'—
Could the divine plan include such incendiary agents?
'Did he who made the Lamb make thee?'

Blake communed with the tigers, fed on dogs and dead horses,
And cruelly taunted by their visitors;
Incarcerated in the Tower, full of instruments of torture
And eerily populated by headless spectres.

Then fixated by the lustrous blaze that still flashed from their eyes
Blake wrote that 'The tigers of wrath
Are wiser than the horses of instruction'—a visionary epigram
Urging man to fight for unbridled freedom.

Blake meant those filled with righteous anger, following their
    desires,
Were wiser than those taking instruction from others' rules
Or, as both the Grateful Dead and Joe Strummer chose to emblazon
In red letters on subversive guitars, IGNORE ALIEN ORDERS.

In another age of revolution Blake's words on man's wrathful
    wisdom
Would resurface as a popular graffiti,
Being transcribed by a Situationist group called King Mob Echo
Next to ALL YOU NEED IS DYNAMITE.

And nearby was written RENT REVOLT, suggesting how human
    beings
Might be also maddened by their social confinement:
Caged by poverty traps; unjustly hobbled, their horizons
    narrowed,
And snarling at those whom they held responsible.

In 1903, Calcutta Zoo kept a Bengali tiger behind bars;
A demonized man-eater of whom stereoscopic views
In sepia tints were sold for people to be titillated by fear,
While they'd enjoy the Empire's creature comforts.

This Bengali tiger had eaten over 220 human beings,
Some being mauled to death in tea plantations—
Its other victims wrenched out of hides in the jungle
From where hunters had been taking potshots.

'*Did he who made the Lamb make thee?*' Blake enquired,
Puzzled by his God devising such untrammelled wildness—
The same sabre-toothed spirit that Shiva's seen mounted on,
A depiction of the immortally and savagely irrepressible.

'*Did he who made the Lamb make thee?*' Blake asked,
Addressing himself to the celestial blacksmith
Who'd forged muscles which gave tigers the kind of heart
That urged them to devour deer and to snack on men,

And rip crocodiles' eyes from their sockets like sweets.
What explained a creature of such unparalleled ferocity?
Why did he plan for it to tear so unrestrainedly into flesh?
Might he just relish the insolent skills he'd imagined for it?

For this dread creature that's described as having no off-switch,
And which Henry V would urge his troops to emulate
At daybreak before the battle of Harfleur: 'When the blast of war
Blows in our ears, then imitate the action of the tiger:

'Stiffen the sinews, summon up the blood...then lend the eye
A terrible aspect...Now set the teeth
And stretch the nostril wide, hold hard the breath and bend up
Every spirit to his full height.'

'The tiger fierce,' Blake noted, 'laughs at the human form.'
And this remained true till man, threatened by its raw energy,
Determined to have the last laugh himself by slowly stealing
The tigers' extensive lands, and then all of its talents.

In Blake's time every tiger alive would have had a territory
Of some 400 square miles in the wild,
Through which it could roam the world as nature's free spirit
Till killing it for sport became a fashion for royalty—

With tiger skins being hung in Maharajahs' palaces,
Carpeting the floors of gangster potentates,
And being laid across Hollywood movie-star beds,
Due to a belief they gave off an erotic charge.

Abattoirs full of bodies betray the excesses of this delusion—
Numberless tigers having had their genitalia removed,
Their male members processed into mystical versions of Viagra
With no man-made 'Year of the Tiger' preventing it.

Most of the tigers in Vietnam have been exterminated;
Those in Java and the Caspian region are extinct—
Thanks to man seeking 'natural' remedies for every ailment
Tigers are trapped then unnaturally commodified.

The medicinal process involves the animals being skinned
And their carcasses stored in freezers;
Their bones are separated then steeped in vats of rice wine—
Herbs are added, plus spurious claims.

A Taiwanese brewery imports 2,000 kilos of tiger bones yearly,
Representing the deaths of some 200 tigers,
Who serve to manufacture 100,000 bottles of 'Tiger Bone Wine',
Each customer told that he can outrun any prey.

Then tiger whiskers 'give courage' and 'protection from bullets'
And reputedly even 'prevent toothache'.
The tigers' eyeballs are rolled into pills to prevent epilepsy
And any other cerebral convulsions.

Tiger meat mixed with oil and rubbed over the body
Will 'cure laziness' and also cure acne.
Its tail 'removes wrinkles' and its heart, once eaten,
Will 'instantly impart strength and cunning'—

Such superstitions spawn 'speed-breeding factory farms'
Where hundreds of farm tigresses
Are induced to cub more frequently than they do in the wild
And forced to bear up to three litters a year.

For the cubs are taken from their mothers before they're weaned
Then made to suckle from other animals such as a dog
Or even a pig—both are used as a tiger's 'wet-nurse surrogates'
And to accelerate the tigresses' production of young.

As the tiger's revered for its strength and sexual prowess,
Old wives' tales lead to its organs being peddled
So that consumers may harness the tiger's powerful stamina
And sexual gourmets pay thousands for a tiger's penis.

They reduce the tiger to being an economic juggernaut's road-kill,
Its body parts displayed hanging from meat hooks . . .
In *The Marriage of Heaven and Hell*, Blake boldly declared
That 'the genitals are beauty', but he couldn't have envisaged

That charlatans, ever eager to exploit the sexually insecure,
And noticing the virile tiger's orgasmic Niagara,
Would then cite 'sympathetic magic' as scientific evidence
For marketing a tiger's genitalia as a quack cure:

'Tiger King sex pills make the penis erect quickly,
Improve sexual intercourse quality,
Shorten the interval for a second intercourse
And they will also reduce fatigue.

'They remove premature ejaculation, activate kidneys,
And increase secretions of testicle cells.
They contain many vigor factors required by the male.
They can increase his spirit, and essence.'

Thus man's flaccid lovemaking requires a tiger be neutered:
Its organs sliced off for an aphrodisiac crutch.
The tiger's penis, so cunningly spined to stimulate ovulation,
Is made into a pill to treat erectile dysfunction.

Incredibly, tigers die to provide men with enriched orgasms
Whose by-product is an increase in human population,
While the tiger's numbers decrease in a depraved equation:
An ancient soul stolen for it to be recycled into sex aids.

In Taiwan captive tigers are executed and their bodies auctioned.
At which dealers stage promotional demonstrations,
Hiring prostitutes and vigorous studs to simulate sensual excess
After ostensibly sampling the products on display.

A seedy hawker in Taipei's Snake Alley night market
Will accost a prospective customer,
'If you drink this, sir, you won't be able to get zipper up.
You forget Viagra, this last you forever.'

A Taizhong restaurant, Pu Chung Pao, serves the island's wealthy
With $20,000 meals in the Ching dynasty style;
These include tiger penises imported from north-east China
Because 'tigers from cold places are better'.

According to the staff: 'We soak them for about a week.
Then when they're soft we start to simmer them.
We add all the types of medicine that are good for men,
While cooking the soup for twenty-four hours.'

When asked if it's popular, the answer's a firm yes—
'Especially among the men in Taiwan.
One tiger penis makes soup for eight people, and it costs
Around 8,000 new Taiwan dollars.'

The idea that tigers may be an endangered species
Is met with an indifferent shrug
For on the black market a highly desired tiger penis
Will attract a price of £3,000.

A dealer says, 'It must be ordered months in advance.
It tastes the same as any other penis might taste,
But, you see, many people in China like to order tiger
Just to show off how much money they have.'

Of the white tigers that bound across Siberian wastes
There may be just ten of them left in the wild—
Ten living Viagra tablets remaining in nature's packet
For that turbid rush of blood over in seconds.

In his poem 'Dreamtigers', Jorge Luis Borges would remember
How he'd once been a 'zealous worshipper of the animal'—
'En la infancia yo ejercí con fervor la adoración del tigre...'
And he'd remember 'the striped, Asiatic, royal tiger'.

Remember, too, how as a child he'd linger near its cage in the zoo
And how he'd judge the gigantic encyclopedias
And natural history books in the library
'According to the majesty of their tigers'.

Then he'd grown up and the tigers, together with his passions,
Grew old, but he'd notice they'd endured in his dreams:
Remarking that, in what he called 'the submerged dimension',
'At that level of the chaotic, they persist.'

'I'm aware,' Borges recounts, 'that this is a dream
And that in a dream my powers are limitless:
My mind can bring a tiger into existence. I cause a tiger,
But it's never the wild beast I remember.'

'Oh how couldst thou deform those beautiful proportions
Of life and person?' Blake would enquire,
Then wrote in his book of prophecy, *The Four Zoas*,
'For as the person, so is his life proportioned.'

Were you to chant 'Tiger, tiger, tiger' a thousand times
You'd have counted each one left in the wild.
Unselfconsciously charismatic; graceful and fearless;
Defiantly independent and each close to death.

'When the stars,' Blake asked, 'threw down their spears,
And watered heaven with their tears,
Did he smile his work to see?
Did he who made the Lamb make thee?'

He did, but Blake's tiger wasn't meant to be farmed or filleted;
Nor its gene pool narrowed down till it stagnated—
Nor its tigerness bred out by being pharmaceutically processed,
With its stripes serving as a ready-made bar code.

Yet two centuries later, in the Sunderbans forest in Bangladesh,
The tiger god, Dakshi Ray, competes with Blake's God—
It's the one place left on earth where the tigers are multiplying
Thanks to the cyclones due to man-made climate change.

The cyclones fill the rivers with bodies for tigers to scavenge;
Now there are tigers which will eat only human meat.
All forest visitors wear tiger masks on the backs of their heads
To stop attacks from behind, but the tactic has little effect.

For in the Sunderbans the tiger's at the top of the food chain,
Biting into a man's neck, then breaking his spine—
Man can turn his back on nature and become dead to karma
Only to find his own body parts restoring a tiger's spirits.

In the age of Kali Yuga, the present age of destruction,
To 'ride the tiger' becomes crucial in challenging it;
And to dream of 'flying on a tiger's back' renews courage—
Thoughts that will prove impotent if tigers are ghosts.

When Blake died, his friend George Richmond of Half Moon
    Street
Closed Blake's eyes, saying he was doing it 'to keep the vision in'—
A vision that's there in the aether—a glimpse of an immortal
    Tiger,
Burning bright in man's being and in the forests of the night.

GHOSTS

Sir Oliver Lodge
Made the first transmission
Across the aether.

He used radio waves
Some months before Marconi,
Yet he's forgotten

Due to his dabbling in
Spiritualism. Lodge
Also used radio

To try to contact
Several spirits of the dead
In Oxford graveyards,

And was denounced as
A crank and discredited.
Few have heard of him

Though he has a plaque
In the Oxford Museum
Lecture theatre,

Where he broadcast.
Lodge might be transmitting now,
To correct history—

Though his being dead
Would weaken the signal, but
You'd need no licence

To listen to Lodge
While he set the record straight
From beyond the grave.

Coincidentally,
His rival, Marconi, would
Also spend years

Trying to perfect
An electrical device
That would establish

Permanent contacts
Between this world and the next
On shortwave radio.

Devoutly Catholic,
He'd thought the first radio sounds
Were voices of the dead

And later believed that
You could pick up messages
From the past, still here.

He would even claim
That he could pick up Christ's words,
As Christ was dying.

John Logie Baird thought
'Important and far-reaching
Discoveries lay

'In waiting', in his words,
'On these discredited paths
And in the shadows.'

W. B. Yeats
Would visit a charlatan
In Leamington Spa

Through whose 'necrophone'
Yeats could contact his dead wife—
If he paid a fee.

The suggestive sounds
From the necrophone ensured
His frequent return.

Marvell wrote: 'The grave's
A fine and private place, but
None . . . do there embrace.'

Yeats's necrophone
Could have introduced Marvell
To telephone sex.

Rudyard Kipling thought
That he could visit John Keats
While Keats was writing

'St. Agnes's Eve'
And in this way feel the things
That Keats was feeling—

Given a wireless
That had been specially tuned
To old poetry.

Arthur Conan Doyle,
The man who wrote Sherlock Holmes,
Believed in fairies

And when two small girls
From Cottingley near Bradford
Cut out some fairies

From a magazine
And mounted them on cardboard
Then stuck them on hatpins

To photograph them,
Doyle forgot Holmes's sleuthing skills
And pronounced them real.

In 1921
The *New York Times* reported
Thomas Edison

To be working on
A machine to measure the
Hundred trillion

'Life units' he claimed
That 'may scatter after death'.
Edison spent years

Trying to construct
A machine to track these down
In the here and now.

He thought it would bring
Comfort to war widows if
Their husbands lived on.

He told the paper:
'These little entities of
Personality

'I hope to detect
With my apparatus are
Still animal entities.

'Who created them
Or where they go afterwards
I am uncertain.

'I surmise that they
Take up residence elsewhere,
But where I don't know.'

Unfortunately
Edison's light was turned out
Just like everyone's

So his 'life units'—
His hereafter particles—
Remain in the dark.

Houdini spent years
Exposing fraudulent or
False mediums—

Their ectoplasm
And their table-turning and their
Crystal-ball gazing.

Houdini's now dead
But at séances still proves
It's Houdini whom

Some spirit medium
Is claiming to be contacting
By saying, *'I'm fake.'*

WASP HONEY

'Every one hates wasps,' people insist with self-righteous fury
As if anyone who thought otherwise was beyond reason:
'What on earth was God doing making wasps?' a child exclaims,
At a picnic or in a kitchen, or anywhere. 'We hate them.'

The child passionately implies that the whole of creation's at fault
Because of this unwelcome bug in the system. 'Oh go away!
Why are they so annoying? What use are they? And they sting!
You're horrible. You're completely pointless. So just go.'

'Okay, I've told you; now you've had it,' and someone kills one
And, as if in a self-fulfilling prophecy, someone gets stung—
For a threatened wasp's signal, if it should be picked up by its
      fellows,
Urges them to come to its defence, whereupon they attack.

Wasps then leave to pollinate a wild orchid, their speciality, or to
      farm aphids
For honeydew; or to make their waterproof paper nests—
This latter skill giving the Chinese the idea of turning chewed
      pulp into paper
According to Needham's *Science and Civilization in China*.

This biomimetic act, or plagiarism, changed the course of history:
Without the wasp, paper might have been a rarity
And communication confined to papyrus or cuneiform marks
On mud and wax tablets or graveyard inscriptions.

'I still hate them,' the voice persists. 'It doesn't matter what you say,
They're hateful. Absolutely everybody sensible knows that . . .'
After the Falklands (which Borges said was like two bald men
Squabbling over a comb), I was in a library in Buenos Aires—

The library of the University on the banks of the River Plate
Which had been trashed by the Argentine junta.
Everything was still in disarray: books strewn about the floor;
Journals trampled, torn, and out of sequence.

'This is what happened when we had our meetings here,' said Ana
    Cordoba.
'They'd burst in. Then they'd throw red paint at us and leave.'
She pointed to the telltale traces: glossy red drips on books and
    metal shelving.
'Then they'd watch us when we left the library buildings.

'They would know who'd been attending the meetings, you see,
Because of indelible splashes of paint on us. They took us in.
Then we were locked up and . . . tortured. Some people died.
So you mustn't talk to any of the police here, whatever you do.

'You know Eduardo? What they did to him? They bribed a boy
To run past him quickly. Plant something on him incriminating.
Then they arrest Eduardo. Take him to a place in the *villa miseria*.
Looks like a police station, but it's not a police station. It's a fake.

'Total fake. Set up specially for police robbery. *What you got, señor?*
Money? Credit cards? We take them, then we let you go. Maybe.'
Then she added darkly, 'If you're lucky, they don't have bad fun
    with you.
They're not what they seem. They sting you. Worse than your wasp.'

Her city was a place where people persistently stung each other.
Seeing a beautiful woman through the peephole in his door
A friend responded, only to have three men enter, one with a
    machete—
Its blade pressed on his genitals till he gave them his money.

In England I'd once seen a striking picture of a South American
    wasps' nest
In a Victorian book on unusual habitations of the world's wildlife.
The spiky nest hung from a tree and was covered in fierce protrusions
Shaped like inch-long thorns, seemingly to protect the contents.

Remarkable haunting contents I'd not heard of before: this wasp
   made honey.
Its weird nest belonged to a species called *Polybia scutellaris*
Which was only found on the Argentine pampas in its pendulous
   paper castles.
The honey was said to be almost solid, and black as obsidian.

'Did you find any articles yet?' Ana asked, after more time in the
   library,
Studying the remains of painstakingly comprehensive journals
Relating to her country's flora and fauna before the place was
   rubbished
By Galtieri's junta, and indirectly by the wasp-woman Thatcher.

Two centuries before, Dr. Johnson had expressed wiser thoughts
   than theirs
About the Falklands: he'd said that there were just and unjust wars,
And wars which were just not worth fighting, and that the
   Falklands
Fell into the latter category, being the sovereign domain of sheep.

In 200 years little had been learnt. People still hated people
And people still hated wasps, to no useful purpose.
If it was more widely known that wasps made honey
They'd be seen in a different light, and redeemed.

The first account of it by the naturalist Don Félix de Azara was
   ridiculed
As 'a pure concoction of the Baron Munchausen class'.
Undeterred Azara sent a wasps' nest to London, to the British
   Museum,
Where a Dr. Adam White found dry honey in its combs.

So if wasps, with their angry masks, make something as sweet as
   honey
And disrupt the rigour of scientists' categories,
How does it taste? Does it cure stings? Like dock leaves and
   nettles—
Might it even allay the fear of wasps, namely *spheksophobia*?

Then if one wasp can make honey why don't all wasps make honey
And improve their public standing?
Perhaps this one's a mutant species designed not to die off like
    bees?
A hardcore hymenopteran producing punk honey;

As bees are dying off (thanks, it would seem, to global pollution,
With smog interfering with the bee's ability to find nectar)
Then this steelier wasp might be replacing its lovable hippy
    cousin
By manufacturing the sweetest stuff that life has to offer.

When I chanced to unearth a metallic wasp, near where I'd
    ended up,
One which had a transparent abdomen like a portable honeypot
With antennae-like reindeer antlers looking more than usually
    alien,
Its outlandishness suggested that wasps were capable of anything.

Then Jorge Godoy told me of a Guaraní Indian in the north-east,
On the borders of Paraguay, in the region of Gran Chaco.
'He knows the biography of every blade of grass. So he'll know.
He speaks good Spanish . . . Guaraní means forest people.'

Originally they came from the Amazon basin seven centuries ago
To look for *Iwy Mara' Eye*, 'a land without evil'.
They were guided by their prophets, wearing their sacred feathers,
And by their *Ava Yumpa*, which means 'God man'.

Jorge and I travelled to meet Manu on a tributary of the Río Paraná.
He greeted us with a brief word, sucked on his *maté* gourd,
Then fell silent. 'The spikes on the nest,' I asked, 'of the
    camoati'—
The indigenous name—'they're protection from jaguars?'

Manu looked puzzled. I opened the book I'd brought to show him,
The Romance of Animal Arts and Crafts,
With its picture of a wasps' nest attacked by a snarling jungle cat
And the swarm of honey-wasps defending it.

Manu furrowed his brow. '*No. Para ventilar. Caliente aqui.*'
The book evidently overdramatized the nest's spikes—
They were there simply to ventilate the nest and keep it cool.
He grinned. 'I'm more danger to this wasp than a cat.'

He explained this was because the *camoati* honey made him feel
    good
And when he felt good this reduced his hatred
For those who'd stolen his land: Brazilians, Bolivians, North
    Americans
And Paraguayans. It was a consuming hatred.

The *pytagua*, or foreigners, had edged him from the land he'd
    inhabited
For generations, reducing his people to living by roadsides,
But when he saw the wasp's spiny fortress he could still feel
    happy,
For it held one secret which sustained him.

It was that 'even this wicked wasp, he has learnt to make honey,
And the wasp has to do this—despite his bad nature—
Because all those who want to live have to be good in some
    way,
But you must learn how to discover this goodness.'

He climbed up to prise clear a tiny portion of the elusive comb.
'I borrow a little for you. I don't steal. It's their honey.'
A squad of black creatures moved out of their thorny scrotal sac
To crawl all over him during this suspenseful inspection.

A surviving article in the library had spoken of Guaraní wasp-
    honey shamans
Who make a 'mouth music' while collecting it and are never
    stung.
'They know I already have "mad honey disease",' Manu laughed
    at our concern.
Then he turned back to continue delving while he vibrantly
    hummed.

'These wasps feed on jimson weed. So their honey contains
    atropine—
It lets you know how you're going to die.' He handed us some comb
Then he added, out of the blue, 'Stupid people cause a lot of
    damage. Why?'
'Will this cure them?' I asked. 'I'm still testing it,' he smiled.

It tasted strange, this counterintuitive honey produced by creatures
The world always feels justified in so intractably hating...
An intriguing after-effect was an old enemy buzzing my
    consciousness.
He appeared to lean forward, to smile gently, then wave.

Darwin made many references to the work of Don Azara,
To his studies of woodpeckers and black-necked swans,
And the five hundred other birds of Argentina's River Plate
That Don Azara had captured and then pickled in brandy.

Darwin also drew on Azara's studies of small Indian tribes
And on their methods of sexual selection:
Researches that found their way into Darwin's *Descent of Man*
And would fuel fascist doctrines of the survival of the fittest.

Oddly, however, Darwin overlooked Azara's discovery
Of *Polybia scutellaris*, the honey-producing wasp—
Still inconceivable to those who like things cut and dried,
To whom wasps are evil and cannot make anything good.

★

On returning to Buenos Aires I bought a new blank book,
A black Moleskine, and made a whimsical note
Of the irony that man's intellectual dependence on paper
Had made him a kind of Mowgli—civilized by wasps.

In San Telmo market, a frail ailing couple with a wind-up
    gramophone
Elegantly tango to *Milonga de mis amores*—
Both parents of a young boy on the *Belgrano*, torpedoed by the
    British,
They collect money by telling strangers their story.

I see a graffiti, LAS MALVINAS SON ARGENTINAS, at La Recoleta
    Cemetery,
Where a family's mausoleum has electricity, so the bereaved
May boil a kettle and spend the day playing their loved one
    records.
The war graves show a human wasp's sting lasts the longest.

THE EVOLUTION OF DARWIN'S HEAD

There will be no justice as long as man will stand with a gun and destroy those who are weaker than he is.
  —Isaac Bashevis Singer (1902–1991)

In his autobiography Charles Darwin looks back
And realizes how his love for science
'Gradually preponderated', as he puts it,
'Over every other taste'.

But initially Darwin kept up his other passions,
In particular for shooting,
Which persisted, as Darwin says of himself,
'In nearly full force' until he'd shot

Almost all the birds and animals that he needed
For his collection on board the *Beagle*.
Then slowly shooting would interfere with his work
And Darwin gave up his gun, forever.

He'd been obsessed with shooting since childhood.
'I do not believe that any one,' Darwin recalled,
'Could have shown more zeal for the most holy cause
Than I did for shooting birds.

'How well I remember killing my first snipe,
And my excitement was so great
That I had much difficulty in reloading my gun
From the trembling of my hands.

'How I did enjoy shooting! But I think that I must
Have been half-consciously ashamed of my zeal,
For I tried to persuade myself that shooting
Was almost an intellectual employment.

'It required so much skill to judge where to find most game
And to hunt the dogs well.
My taste long continued. Though, to my deep mortification,
My father once said to me . . .'

And here he relived Dr. Darwin's great anger:
You care for nothing but shooting, dogs, and rat-catching,
And you'll be a disgrace, his father had declared,
To yourself and to the rest of your family.

But later, on giving up his gun, Darwin discovered
That 'the pleasure of observing and reasoning
Was a much higher one than that of skill and sport'.
Then, in an aside—apocalyptic for gun lovers—

Darwin suggests that his change of heart was so radical
It caused a change in his physical appearance—
In other words that he, Darwin, actually metamorphosed.
He recounts what had happened on his return from the voyage:

'That my mind,' Darwin explained, 'became developed
Through my pursuits during the voyage
Is rendered probable by a remark made by my father,
Who was the most acute observer I ever saw,

'My father was a man of a skeptical disposition
And far from being a believer in phrenology,
But on first seeing me after the voyage
He turned round to my sisters and exclaimed:

'*Why, the shape of his head is quite altered.*'
These were Darwin's father's exact words.
Darwin was recognizable, but for his changed head—
As if giving up his gun had made it mutate.

After the claim his son's head was now very different
Neither he nor Darwin provides any more detail—
But if this change had transformed Darwin into a monster
Then it's likely it was noticed by witnesses.

Yet, if the opposite was the case, as is more likely,
And his son's looks had become more pleasing
Then the transformation of Darwin's head is a game-changer—
A paradigm shift which rivals man's descent from apes.

For just as with Alice, in 'Alice in Wonderland',
When her body grew larger, or when it shrank,
Charles Darwin's long-overlooked evolutionary spurt
Has to provide man with a whole new perspective.

It's an odd quirk of social evolution that both gun nuts
And the military should appear bullet-headed:
They're shorn and thin-lipped with an alienating look;
Hostile, aggressive, and darkly threatening

As if hell-bent on creating a self-selecting stereotype
By their stamping and strutting about in fatigues—
Speaking in a machine-gun staccato, *On the floor, asshole!*
And killing anyone, quite untroubled by second thoughts.

Their stirred-up hatred is expressed in stylized expletives—
Die, motherfuckers! Snuff 'em! Waste 'em! —
Spat out in metallic voices to mask any signs of fear,
Along with the grim lifelessness that passes for 'cool'.

With an all-consuming avarice the US has profited
From pioneering the entertainment value of guns:
Its video games now allow you to kill hundreds every hour
While its real-life gun deaths are thought normal.

A week after a man opened fire in a Tucson car park,
Leaving six people dead and thirteen wounded,
The Crossroads of the West gun show rolled into town—
And sold out of the same Glock 9-millimetre just used.

Crossroads gun shows have 600,000 visitors a year.
A *My First Rifle* made by Crickett is popular.
It's a working version of Daddy's gun for four- to ten-year-olds
And it comes in pink or black for $140.

Such mass conformity is approved of by US luminaries:
The movie star Arnold Schwarzenegger
Has swaggeringly stated, 'I have a love interest
In every one of my films: it's a gun.'

Charlton Heston was also married to a gun and if anyone
Threatened to separate the happy couple
By taking his toy, he'd promise them five chilling words:
'From my cold dead hands.'

Then when their President was challenged—
After Lennon had just been shot dead in New York—
About the US's psychopathic passion for its guns,
Reagan said the US was still 'howdy doody'.

But imagine, for a second, if, thanks to Darwin's hint
In his *Recollections of the Development of My Mind and Character*,
His autobiographical field notes of 1876,
There's a previously unidentified evolutionary force

Which ensures that by giving up guns you get a makeover . . .
Imagine if all of those following in Darwin's footsteps
Were now able to reproduce this evolutionary change
And mysteriously acquire a more pleasing look.

What if, instead of seeking selfish thrills from someone's dying—
Spewing blood in a sadistic spray of man's bullets—
It dawns on him that it could be more fun to spend time
Working out how the world's put together?

In a youthful portrait Darwin looks notably suspicious:
He's frowning and even seems faintly criminal.
But later, when the passion for killing's cast aside,
His looks are benign and engagingly congenial—

This 'before and after' evidence that guns are bad for the
    appearance
Makes you wonder if the so-called 'right to bear arms'
In the US Constitution, which bullies insist is Holy Writ,
Doesn't amount to Natural Selection by Ugly Americans,

For whom gun worship is really a sorry form of self-harm,
For despite its proud citizens owning millions of guns,
Each gun stops them from escaping their armed cul-de-sac
And embracing the survival of the friendliest.

'Nothing will end war unless people themselves,'
Einstein would say, 'refuse to go to war.'
'If my soldiers were to think,' echoed Frederick the Great,
'Not one of them would remain in the army.'

'Man has no right to kill his brother,' Shelley asserted.
'It is no excuse that he does so in uniform
For by his doing so, he only adds the infamy
Of servitude to the crime of murder.'

Whoever may doubt that a backlog of fetish behaviour
By those spending years fondling their guns
Can have spawned mutants with wayward trigger fingers
And maybe even hideously bullet-shaped heads

Forgets that someone who once threw away his gun
Suddenly found that he'd grown a new mind—
One that helped him change the world for the better
And made him nicer-looking as a result.

Also, despite received wisdom, Darwin said:
It wasn't the strongest of the species which survives
But 'the one that is the most adaptable to change',
And guns certainly outlive their survival value.

When his 38-calibre revolver failed to fire at his intended victim
During a hold-up in Long Beach, California,
A would-be robber called James Elliot peered down the barrel
And tried the trigger again. This time it worked.

Darwin the studious rationalist spells it out clearly
In this graphic account of his life,
Namely as soon as he gave up his compulsion for killing
It changed the very shape of his organ of thought—

Yet it was Darwin's other themes that grabbed headlines,
Namely that man had come from apes
And that the world took longer than six days to make,
Disproving the Bible's account in Genesis;

And that man's notions of a supreme power were irrelevant
Either to the Earth's origins or to its future—
Despite creationists invoking God to destroy Darwin
And praying that their vengeful God end his world.

But Darwin's agnostic ghost, with its head made of dust
In an attractive arrangement, may be whispering:
'Guns are crap! Be prettier! Change for the better!'
And might welcome Darwin's remedy getting exposure—

Whereby the 200 million unlovely American gun nuts
Can be beautified along with others worldwide—
Without having to pay thousands for cosmetic surgery
Since each may alter their looks just by thinking.

Christopher Walken, the actor, once hearteningly sowed
A fresh seed in the American psyche:
'I don't even like holding them. Whenever I hold a gun,
I want to get it out of my hand as quick as possible.'[1]

So perhaps when Darwin's formula for man's future
Has taken over the entire human gene pool
Then the last attention-seeking bore waving a gun
Will be ignored like a dull drunk in a bar.

'For it's never the job of thinking people
To side with the executioners,'
Said Camus, and Oscar Wilde backed him up:
'War's weapons aren't wicked, just vulgar.'

Yet US gun lobbies persist: 'Guns don't kill people,
It's people that kill people, stupid—
Or are you gonna blame pencils for misspelling, dumbass . . . ?'
No . . . but when zillions of aeons

Have evolved a sophisticated biocomputer,
Homo sapiens, with its infinite brain—
This groundbreaking entity that enables a planet
To attain a measure of self-awareness—

Only the shallow would attack one at random
As it emerges from its long assembly line—
Then smash it from their compulsion to take life
Before they're able to master life's manual.

When coming to this last verse in June 2011,
I saw a stencilled slogan on the pavement
That said all of this in four words in red paint.
Its message read: 'Killing people is rude.'

The US has 500 million guns in private hands
And states outlawing Darwin's teaching.
The US devours a million animals every hour,
And it shows no sign at all of changing—

But if all of its guns and its gun movies were yawned at
And if no animals were processed into American fat,
And if scientific observation replaced bigoted faith
The Ugly American would prove a prettier sight.

Notes

1. Christopher Walken, *Entertainment Weekly*, 17 March 2001.

ALL BIKES ARE WEAPONS

Bicycling is the nearest approximation I know to the flight of birds. The airplane simply carries a man on its back like an obedient Pegasus; it gives him no wings of his own.
  —Louis J. Halle (1910–1998)

All bikes are weapons:
Making cyclists warriors
Who kick pollution
With their miracle
Machines that rectify greed.
Revolutionary—
Wheels spinning around
Trillions and trillions of times
On an empty tank.
Just an airy lungful
Pumped tightly into two tubes,
Causing nothing but
Exhilaration
And liberation, instead of
Trails of death and filth.
On their bikes, wise clowns
Keep pneumatic hoops gyrating
In perfect balance.
Oil rigs aren't blown up.
There's no spillage in the seas
From bicycle wars.
The business oil giant,
Shell, makes £1.6 million
Every hour:
Poisonous profits,
Whose balance sheets unbalance

Every step you take.
Bicycle power
Produces no exhaust fumes.
No carcinogens.
Man-powered machines
Are anti-capitalist—
You can't meter air.
The bicycle is
The most efficient machine
Ever created.
Stored-up calories
Become gas: three thousand
Miles per gallon.
Bikes are subversive:
'Governments must help get rid
Of cars so that bikes
Can eliminate
Government,' Dutch anarchists
Wrote in Amsterdam.
Few are unhappy
On bikes. Everyone's angry
Trapped in deadly cars.
On a recumbent
Bike the top speed is
A hundred and thirty-
Two kilometres
Per hour which, by rights, should make
Oil quite redundant.
While big oil clings to
Motorized suicide-bombs
For man's transport,
Revolving bike wheels
Postpone the end of the world—
Second by second.
'Nothing compares to
The simple pleasure of a
Bike ride.' J.F.K.

If he'd stuck to bikes
And ignored Dallas limos
He'd have lived longer.
What a decision!
'Bicycles run on fat and
They save you money.
Cars run on money
And they make you fat.'
This graffiti
In San Francisco presents
An obvious choice . . .
Be bottled-up wasps—
Abusing fellow drivers
And squirting poison—
Or restore balance
By mounting a naked bike:
Fun between your legs.

X-RAY DEATH

'I'm looking at my own death,' Bertha Röntgen said,
Glimpsing the jointed bones inside her fingers.
Wilhelm Röntgen had led her towards his X-ray tube,
Taking her by the hand—but not in order to kiss it.

After impregnating it with a dose of ionizing radiation
He imprinted its image on a photographic plate
So that his wife could see through her skin to her digits—
Like spindly witches' hats in a fluorescent mist.

When γνῶθι σεαυτόν was written above the oracle at Delphi
You needed a lifetime to attain self-awareness.
Now, thanks to Herr Röntgen's X-rays, this became instant:
'*Look, there's my ribcage . . . my spine . . . my skull!*'

Unfortunately, to know oneself proved dangerous.
Exposure to the radiation caused blisters, burns,
And grisly cancers, requiring limbs be amputated:
Röntgen's assistant, Clarence Dally, lost his arms.

Dally couldn't carve his Christmas turkey,
Nor hold on to his wife as they made love,
Nor close his hands to pray when his time was up,
Though Dally still knew himself inside out.

The X-ray machine caught on. Now it's in airports,
For trapping those with explosives in their clothes.
Yet an abiding terrorist continues to evade capture:
With his X-ray eyes he watches skeletons dance.

Since your birth he has stalked you with a radiant grin,
Snatching frames for the darkest darkroom,
Then forcing you to keep dead still for the final exposure,
Cackling coldly as he snaps you—only to fog the film.

ACKNOWLEDGEMENTS

Eddie Mizzi, Sophie Huxley, Dave Motion, Jonangus Mackay, Stephanie and Alastair Pirrie, Simon Drake, Lutz Kroth, Terry Stewart, Carl Williams, Sarah Murphy, Adrian Arbib, Martin Maw, Dave and Di Nelstrop, Diana Senior, Claire Palmer, Carl Williams, Charles Boyle, Malcolm Ritchie, Roy Hutchins, Dave Lawton, Martin Wilkinson, Lily Williams, Jorge Torres de Zabaleta, Lisa Wolfe, Gabriella F. Ruellan, Zhao Xiang-Ning, Han Wei-Lian, Nigel Allen, P. St. G., Tony Simcock, Lesley Levene, Elena Caldera, P. J. Smith, *sine quibus non.*

Also available from Huxley Scientific Press:

The Oxford Science Walk, by Sophie Huxley
Darwin's Mysterious Illness, by Robert Youngson
Oxford Trees (2nd edition), by Sophie Huxley
Penicillin and Luck, by Norman Heatley
Eric Gill in Oxford, by Sophie Huxley
Aristotle, the Market Place, and the Idea of a University,
by George Huxley